The distinctive 'Liverpool special' was made in 1863. The only one still in use is in Shiel Road, Liverpool. Another one, not in use, is outside Liverpool Head Post Office.

OLD LETTER BOXES

Martin Robinson

Shire Publications Ltd

CONTENTS

Set in 9 point Times roman and printed in Great Britain by C. I. Thomas & Sons (Haverfordwest) Ltd, Press Buildings, Merlins Bridge, Haverfordwest, Dyfed.

British Library Cataloguing in Publication Data available.

All photographs are by the author.

COVER: *Early non-standard pillar box at Barnes Cross, near Sherborne, Dorset.*

LEFT: *Only photographs and odd parts survive of the first London boxes of 1855, made by H. and M. D. Grissell of Hoxton. The public found them both puzzling and amusing.*

Private posting boxes in an Oxford college. The 'post office' aperture is next to the one for letters to be carried by the colleges' private messenger service.

INTRODUCTION

Britain's first roadside letter boxes appeared in 1852 and since that time there have been hundreds of different varieties: pillar boxes, wall boxes of various kinds and lamp boxes, each in different sizes and bearing the ciphers of different sovereigns from Victoria to Elizabeth II. Improvements and changes in style continue to be made up to the present day.

From 1852 to 1859 pillar boxes of various designs were ordered by Post Office District Surveyors for their own areas. From 1859 standard pillar boxes were made for use throughout the United Kingdom, including the hexagonal Penfold design. From 1887 improved versions of the cylindrical pillar box were introduced and these have lasted through subsequent reigns and changes of manufacturer, with a number of small improvements, until the present time. There was some experiment in the reign of George V and again after 1968.

Wall letter boxes first appeared in 1857 and went through a number of modifications until the later Victorian types reached what are recognisably the same designs as the current ones. There are a

great many variations in detail, however, with different ciphers, manufacturers' names, aperture and hood sizes, and so on. Ludlow wall boxes with their distinctive enamel plates were made for use at sub-post offices between 1885 and 1965.

The last of the main types, the lamp boxes, first appeared in 1896. They are found attached to poles, mounted on metal stands or built into convenient walls and they underwent important design changes in 1935 and 1940, as well as a number of changes of detail and manufacturer.

Whenever a new sovereign accedes to the throne a new royal cipher is used, but older letter boxes remain in service, and with very few exceptions there are survivors of all types from the very earliest. Many boxes are still in service at their original locations, whilst others have been recovered and preserved in museums, private collections or in the Post Office's own collection, which it is hoped will one day be placed on public display. There are over a hundred museums which have at least one old letter box, but none has an extensive collection.

LEFT: *This Channel Islands box of 1852 stands outside Post Office Regional Headquarters in Bristol. It was presented by the Guernsey Post Office in 1969 when it became an independent board.*
RIGHT: *This 1853 pillar box, the oldest still in use on the British mainland, stands by an isolated cottage at Barnes Cross near Sherborne in Dorset.*

VICTORIAN PILLAR BOXES

EARLY NON-STANDARD

The earliest pillar boxes in the British Isles were those erected in the Channel Islands in 1852 at the suggestion of Anthony Trollope, the novelist, who was a Post Office Surveyor. One of these is still in use at Union Street, St Peter Port, Guernsey, whilst the only other survivor is at South-west Postal Region Headquarters in Bristol.

The oldest pillar box in daily use on the British mainland is in Dorset. It is one of the boxes made by John Butt of Gloucester, whose nameplate appears on either side of the posting aperture, for the west

of England in 1853-6. At this period District Surveyors were responsible for designing and ordering their own pillar boxes, and whilst the ones made in 1856 for the Eastern District are similar to those in the west of England, those made in 1853 for the north of England and Ireland are quite different, being square, surmounted by a crown and with a horizontal posting aperture. A unique example is preserved at the National Museum, Dublin. The vertical aperture was more usual at the time as it was believed this would make it more difficult to steal letters from the boxes.

In 1856 a most unusual pillar box made its appearance: three samples had been ordered for the Birmingham and Southern District. The box was cast in the form of a fluted column but by a misunderstanding the dome and crown on top were so large that they made the box 8 feet (2.4m) high. In spite of this two of the boxes went into service and one survives in the Post Office's collection. Later the same year further fluted boxes were made but the dome was replaced by a more modest flattened cone. Ten of these survive, of which eight are still in use. In 1857 the box was redesigned with a slightly protruding horizontal aperture and since then all letter boxes have had horizontal apertures, presumably because the vertical aperture had not proved to be any more secure and was more likely to let in the rain.

Suttie and Company of Greenock made some distinctive pillar boxes surmounted by a large crown for use in Scotland in 1856, and one is in the Post Office's collection. In London, meanwhile, six pillar boxes made by H. and M. D. Grissell had been erected in 1855. They were rectangular and about 5 feet (1.5m) tall, the top being surmounted by

LEFT: *An 1856 pillar box made by Andrew Handyside of Derby for the Post Office's Eastern District; one of two surviving at Framlingham, Suffolk. Like many early pillar boxes it has a vertical aperture.*

RIGHT: *An 8 foot (2.4 m) high fluted pillar box made by Smith and Hawkes in 1856. The large domed top, cushion and crown came about as a result of a misunderstanding of the specifications.*

LEFT: *The corrected version of the fluted pillar box, with a flattened conical top and vertical aperture, was also made in 1856. Ten survive; this one is outside the Williamson Art Gallery in Birkenhead.*

RIGHT: *In 1857 the aperture was changed from vertical to horizontal. Only four of these fluted boxes still exist, three of them in Malvern. This one is by Link Common on Worcester Road.*

an iron ball, and they were not well received by the public. In view of this dissatisfaction the Post Office, in collaboration with the Government's Department of Science and Art, designed a completely new box, fifty of which were made by Smith and Hawkes in 1857. The boxes were cylindrical with elaborate mouldings, and the posting aperture was under a flap in the roof. Some were installed in London and others went to provincial cities. The Post Office still has two, one of which is often on display, and there is a third at the Salford Museum.

EARLY STANDARD PILLARS

In order to standardise pillar boxes throughout Britain and Ireland the Post Office decided in 1857 that a cheaper version of the London ornate box, bereft of all the earlier ornamentation, should be made for use in all regions. The only survivor is still in use at the Kent railway station in Cork, Irish Republic. A plate giving collection times was added; on earlier boxes this was displayed separately.

Another design which took account of some criticisms was put out to tender and in 1859 Cochrane and Company began making what are called the 'first national standard' pillar boxes. The design was similar to the cheaper version of the London ornate box, except that the new box was taller, the posting aperture was below the cap and had an inward-opening flap which could not be left open. A wire guard inside stopped letters falling out when the door was opened and the door was hinged at the left instead of the right. The box was supplied in two sizes; there are four surviving examples of the large 'A' size, one of which is in Montpellier

LEFT: Fifty ornate pillar boxes, decorated with masks and festoons of flowers, were made for use in London in 1857. One is in the Salford Museum; the Post Office has two more.

RIGHT: A cheaper version of the ornate box without the decorative mouldings was also made in 1857. The only remaining example is at the Kent railway station, Cork, in the Republic of Ireland.

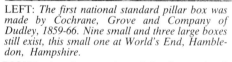

LEFT: *The first national standard pillar box was made by Cochrane, Grove and Company of Dudley, 1859-66. Nine small and three large boxes still exist, this small one at World's End, Hambledon, Hampshire.*

RIGHT: *A unique version of the first national standard pillar with a lamp post on its top can be found by the Co-operative Pioneers Museum in Toad Lane, Rochdale.*

Road, Brighton. The smaller 'B' size can be seen at World's End, Hambledon, Hampshire, and there are three examples in Liverpool.

Even the larger box was found to be insufficient for the volume of mail posted in some parts of Liverpool, and the Postmaster preferred the older method of hanging a mailbag inside rather than the wire guard. He also thought the posting aperture was too small and that the box should bear the words POST OFFICE. In 1863 a few 'Liverpool special' pillar boxes were made by Cochrane. The design was similar to the larger first national standard but there was a crown on top and the words POST OFFICE round the circumference.

LEFT: *Nineteen of the original 1866 Penfolds still exist, of which eight are in Cheltenham, like this one. The aperture just below the top is covered by an enamelled flap.*

RIGHT: *The fourth of the five types of Penfold is the commonest. The aperture is lower and the collection plate has a moulded surround. This example is outside King's College, Cambridge.*

PENFOLDS

Probably the most familiar and best loved of Victorian pillar boxes are those known as Penfolds, which were made between 1866 and 1879. They are named after their designer, the architect J. W. Penfold. Over a hundred of these are in use all over Britain or are preserved in museums. The Penfold is a hexagonal pillar box with the top decorated with acanthus leaves and balls, but there are five distinct types and three sizes, making fifteen possible combinations, of which twelve are known still to exist.

The boxes were made to Penfold's design by Cochrane Grove and Company in 1866. Some of the types are much rarer than others. Only one of the large-size original boxes still exists: it stands, in a neglected condition, in Alcester Road, Studley, Warwickshire. Fourteen of the medium and four of the small size survive.

The original boxes have an inward-opening enamelled flap over the aperture, bearing the word LETTERS, but in about 1871 the Penfolds were adapted by the fitting of an upshoot, which gives the aperture a raised surround. This second type is rare, only six examples being known. The third type was brought about in 1872 by the complaint that letters could be trapped inside the top of the box, so the aperture was lowered to change places with the coat of arms below. Only five examples of this type still exist. The commonest of the Penfolds is the fourth type, introduced soon afterwards. Three main differences from the previous type can be observed: the collection plate now has a moulded surround and has been moved down one inch (25 mm) from the

LEFT: *The 'anonymous' pillar boxes of 1879-87 bear no royal cipher or other wording apart from the maker's name. A few have a raised ring on the top, the reason for which is unknown.*

RIGHT: *A famous anonymous box in Priory Road, Cambridge, is surmounted by fearsome spikes. It probably once stood next to a wall and the spikes were to deter people from climbing over.*

top of the door; the door itself has protruding hinges. There are over sixty survivors, half of which are in London. The fifth and last type has the VR cipher at the top of the door and the collection plate lower down. There are only eight of these left.

ANONYMOUS BOXES

A new cylindrical design was put out to tender in 1878. The new boxes were cast in two sizes and distributed from March 1879. The basic shape and style of this pillar box have remained much the same, with only a few modifications, through six reigns. The pillar boxes made by Handyside between 1879 and 1887 bear no royal cipher, crown or wording of any kind except for the maker's name beneath the door. For this reason they are referred to as 'anonymous' boxes. Over three hundred survive and rather fewer than half this number are the larger 'A' size, most of which are in London.

LEFT: *From 1883 the anonymous pillar boxes were made with the aperture lower to prevent letters becoming trapped out of sight inside the top of the box. This example is in Warwick.*

RIGHT: *Standard pillar boxes from 1887 bore the sovereign's cipher on the door and the words POST OFFICE. A metal strip at the right of the door was to keep out rainwater.*

By 1883 further complaints had been made about letters being trapped inside the top of pillar boxes, and from that year boxes were made with the aperture a few inches lower. These low-aperture anonymous boxes, which were made until 1887, are not as common as those with the high aperture, fewer than two hundred being still in use.

In 1887 the Post Office admitted that there had been an oversight and from then onwards all pillar boxes had the royal cipher VR cast in script letters on the door and the words POST OFFICE on either side of the posting aperture.

In 1889 oval pillar boxes with two apertures to enable 'town' and 'country' letters to be separated were first installed in London. The dual posting scheme was extended to other cities in 1905.

An Edward VII dual-aperture pillar box of 1901 in Grays Inn Road, London. The door with Queen Victoria's cipher must be a replacement from an earlier recovered box.

LEFT: *An airmail box of 1932 at Shoreham Airport, West Sussex, still has its double collection-plate holder, one part of which originally displayed information about airmail rates, the other part collection times.*

RIGHT: *The centre of Birmingham still has some of the short-lived rectangular sheet-steel boxes of 1968. The royal cipher was originally stencilled on the door, and the casting was added later.*

TWENTIETH-CENTURY PILLAR BOXES

When Edward VII came to the throne in 1901 large, small and dual-aperture pillar boxes were cast with his cipher. Two styles of cipher are known: the first and much rarer is called the 'open' type, whilst the second has curled ends to the letters. In 1904 the problem of trapped letters was finally solved by increasing the height of the door and setting the posting aperture within it. The dual-aperture box of Edward VII can be found with ciphers on the doors at each end or with one centrally placed cipher.

During the reign of George V there were three major experiments. In 1930

the Post Office installed special airmail letter boxes in London which offered later posting times for airmail letters than ordinary letter boxes, and also with their distinctive blue livery and prominent AIR MAIL signs they acted as a reminder to the public of the rapidly growing airmail service. In 1936-7 the scheme came to an end when ordinary correspondence was forwarded to Europe and the British Empire without the need for airmail surcharges, and by 1938 the last blue box had gone. A few survive, repainted in red and put into ordinary use. It is possible to identify such a box if it retains its characteristic double collection plate, or perhaps one plate has been removed and the remaining one is off centre.

The two other experiments concern the provision of stamp vending machines in combination with a letter box. In 1924 an experimental telephone kiosk incorporating a stamp machine and letter box was installed at Bath. Following the success of this experiment fifty more kiosks were made in 1929. Only two are still in service, at Warrington and Whitley Bay, and four more are preserved. No more were made after the initial batch because of problems in siting them. Another idea was to incorporate a stamp machine into a pillar box, and in 1932 oval pillars with a posting aperture at one end and a stamp machine at the other were cast by Andrew Handyside, now Derby Castings. Fifty small and 75 large pillars were made; eight small and 25 large ones survive.

During the short reign of Edward VIII 161 pillar boxes were cast, of which many are still in use, although only sixteen of the larger 'A' size are known still to exist. There are many George VI pillar boxes still in use, and since 1952 the cipher of Queen Elizabeth II has been used. Over

LEFT: *A short-lived experiment was made in 1974 with a rectangular cast iron box, but this proved faulty in design and more expensive to cast than the traditional cylinder.*

RIGHT: *Nine examples of the first standard wall letter boxes of 1857 still exist, mostly in the south and west of England. They have no hood over the aperture and the door is in the middle.*

the years there have been small changes, like the adoption of a 10 inch (250 mm) rather than an 8 inch (200 mm) aperture, but more radical experiments still take place. In 1968 two hundred pillar boxes of a revolutionary design were made by Vandyke Engineers of Harlow. These were rectangular and made of steel sheets instead of the traditional cast iron, so that separate panels could be easily replaced. The internal fittings were also completely redesigned. The boxes were installed either singly or in pairs with a common top, but it quickly became apparent that the new boxes could not match the traditional materials or design. In 1974 the Carron Company tried without success to improve on the idea by making a rectangular cast iron box.

In 1980 a completely new design of pillar box was introduced which reverted to the cylindrical shape. These 'K' type boxes have been installed in increasing numbers since then. The earliest castings bear a commemorative plaque on the rear. When pillar boxes of the present reign were erected in Scotland the EIIR cipher proved unacceptable to some Scots because, they argued, the Queen was not Elizabeth II of Scotland, there having been no previous Queen Elizabeth of Scotland. After letter boxes had been painted with tar and even blown up, the Post Office bowed to pressure and since then letter boxes of all types made for Scotland have borne only the Scottish crown with the cipher omitted.

WALL LETTER BOXES

When roadside letter boxes were first introduced in the 1850s they usually served only the populations of towns, where it was thought there would be sufficient use to justify their expense. It rapidly became apparent that smaller letter boxes suitable for villages and other rural sites were needed to meet the growing demand from the public. Specimen boxes were made for the Surveyor of the Western District of England in 1857 and authorisation was given to site them in villages near Plymouth. Unfortunately none of the earliest wall boxes still exists. Meanwhile an iron wall box was made by Smith and Hawkes for the Birmingham District, and after some improvements others were commissioned.

After reports that the boxes were satisfactory and seeing that they cost only a quarter the price of a pillar box 250 more were made by September 1858. Nine of these boxes are still in existence, the best known of which is at the Old Post Office, Tintagel, Cornwall. The box has an inward-opening flap over the horizontal posting aperture; the royal cipher and crown surmount the words CLEARED AT with a space below for a painted collection plate; and the door is in the centre.

Soon rainwater was reported to be finding its way inside through the flap, damaging letters, so an additional casting was suggested which took the form of a small pediment and hood over the aperture. It is believed that about one hundred of the first standard wall boxes were modified in this way, but only eight now survive.

In 1859 Smith and Hawkes were asked to tender for an improved wall box which incorporated the improvements made to the first box and also had a wire guard inside to stop letters falling out when the door was opened. These specifications would make the box twice as expensive, but the manufacturer was prepared to make a smaller, cheaper version which would still have the improvements required. Only one example of what is thought to be the 1859 larger (Number 1) wall box survives, near Wickhambrook in Suffolk, and this rarity seems to testify to its relative unpopularity.

On the other hand by April 1860 500 of the smaller Number 2 boxes had been installed and a hundred more were on order. About sixty of these boxes are still in service around the British Isles. The door is now higher than on the earlier model and the royal cipher, crown and collection plate are set in it. In later versions the hood over the aperture was extended by one inch (25 mm) to give increased protection. One of the Number 2 boxes was sent over to Ireland to be copied by H. and C. Smith of Cork, this being cheaper than importing them from England. A few examples with their signature can still be seen in the Irish Republic.

A few suggestions for improvement were forthcoming from District Surveyors: the boxes should be wider, the keyhole fitted with a protective covering, a doorpull added and something done about the danger of letters lying unseen at the bottom of the box. From 1861 new boxes were made incorporating the improvements suggested, and once more boxes for Ireland were made by H. and

C. Smith. These boxes were supplied for the next ten years, and about twenty of the larger and over one hundred of the smaller types are still in use.

In 1871 further changes were introduced: a larger wall box was made available and designated the 'A' size, the other two sizes becoming 'B' and 'C', and this format has been followed ever since. The size 'A' wall box, nearly 4 feet (1.2 m) high and 20 inches (510 mm) wide, could hold more letters than the largest pillar box but was less than half as expensive to make, so it was thought appropriate for use even in the largest

ABOVE: *A telephone kiosk Number 4 of 1929 incorporating a posting box and two stamp machines. This rare example, formerly in Macclesfield, is now preserved at the Dinting Railway Centre, Glossop, Derbyshire.*

RIGHT: *An experiment of 1932 was an oval pillar box with a posting aperture at one end and a stamp machine at the other. Only eight of the smaller type survive.*

LEFT: *Nearly 150 Edward VIII pillar boxes are still in existence but only sixteen are the larger 'A' size, half of these being in London. This one is in Digbeth, Birmingham.*

BELOW: *This large free-standing wall box which has a pointed roof with a ball is in Battersea, London. A similar one with dual apertures is at Waterloo station, London. Both have the Edward VII 'scroll' cipher.*

towns where suitable walls could be found.

The aperture was changed: the flap and downshoot were replaced by an upshoot, this being thought to be more efficient protection against thieves and rain. The collection plate was repositioned in a recess in the door. Whereas the two smaller sizes were very similar to their predecessors apart from the modifications mentioned, the largest size was unusual in having the words POST OFFICE at the top instead of the royal crown and cipher. The largest size is rare with only half a dozen recorded examples, but the smaller types are much more common.

In 1881 the contract for manufacturing wall letter boxes passed to W. T. Allen and Company. In Allen's boxes the royal cipher and crown always appear at the top with the words POST OFFICE on the hood. The collection plate is mounted on the door in a beading rather than a recess and there is provision for a NEXT COLLECTION tablet in the top right-hand corner of the plate.

Small wall letter boxes of Queen Victoria, Edward VII and George V are sometimes to be found with enlarged apertures. In 1949 a survey showed that

LEFT: *In 1859 the first standard wall box was improved by the addition of a pedimented top and hood to keep out rainwater. This fine example is at Marton, near Welshpool, Powys.*

RIGHT: *The second standard wall box of 1859 incorporated further improvements. This is thought to be the only surviving example of the larger version and stands near Wickhambrook in Suffolk.*

there were 100,000 letter boxes in service which had posting apertures less than 8 inches (200 mm) wide, and there was criticism from the public about the inconvenience of their continued use. By 1956 30,000 such boxes were still in service, mostly in country areas, and a plan was inaugurated to provide one new wall box with a wider aperture in each village. This still left 5,000 boxes to be dealt with, so a contractor was engaged to modify the existing boxes *in situ* by cutting out the aperture and fitting a new casting over it. The programme was carried out between 1959 and 1965, and the effect of the modification is not displeasing.

LEFT: *The smaller version of the second standard wall box is more common. The door is now at the top and holes have been drilled at the bottom to release any water.*

RIGHT: *An example of the Number 1 (large) size of the improved wall box of 1861. The door, with a doorpull, is now at the bottom and the collection plate below the aperture.*

From 1901 wall boxes were made with the cipher of Edward VII, and early versions of the two larger sizes had the cipher ER whereas from later in 1901 to 1904 the cipher included the Roman numerals VII beneath the crown. The earlier types are much rarer. In 1904 a new contract was agreed between the Post Office and W. T. Allen, and some changes were made to the design. Following the alteration made to pillar boxes the door of the largest wall box was enlarged to the full height of the box and the posting aperture set in it. The crown and royal cipher now appear lower down the door and the cipher was redesigned in script style as on the pillar boxes.

The wall letter boxes of George V have a complex history chiefly because, as with the pillar boxes, the contracts passed from one manufacturer to another. New wall letter boxes were introduced: they were intended to be used at post offices and have a door at the back as well as at the front. The boxes are similar to existing ones but have no collection plate and tablet — the collection times would be displayed at the post office window.

After 1930 a larger royal cipher was introduced and the smallest boxes with the large cipher are scarce as they were manufactured for only a year or so. There

LEFT: *A small 1871 wall box. The collection plate is now set in the door. Collection tablets, not originally fitted, were added later in a variety of positions round the door.*

RIGHT: *A small 1881 wall box with aperture modified to 8 inches (200 mm). The aperture was cut away and the new casting fitted in situ. Care was taken not to obscure the royal cipher.*

is also a type of large free-standing wall box with a pointed top surmounted by a ball. The origins of this box are unknown but three examples exist with the cipher of Edward VII or George V.

From the beginning of the reign of George VI only the two larger sizes were made, both with and without collection plates, and the same arrangement still exists. In 1957 it was decided that apertures on all wall boxes made from then on should be increased from 8 inches (200 mm) to 10 inches (250 mm). Also, as with pillar boxes, a special version of the wall box is made for use in Scotland.

LEFT: *A large Edward VII wall box. An earlier version had a larger crown and no VII. From 1904 the large wall box had a full-length door containing the aperture.*

RIGHT: *Only twenty of the small George V wall boxes of 1930 are known. Unlike the more common version, these have a noticeably larger crown and cipher.*

ABOVE: *This old letter box was uncovered at the 'Craven Arms', an old coaching inn at Southam, Warwickshire, which may have been an early letter-receiving house.*

BELOW LEFT: *The old post office at Lyme Regis, Dorset, has this curious letter-posting aperture, which reflects changing opinion about the advisability of horizontal or vertical slots.*

BELOW RIGHT: *A locally made letter box at St Germans, Cornwall, dates from the time when postmasters had to provide their own postboxes. The enamel plate and collection plate have been added later.*

LEFT: *A small Ludlow-type wall box manufactured by the Eagle Range and Foundry Company. This handsome example, still bearing its original enamelled plate, is at Long Street post office, Sherborne, Dorset.*

RIGHT: *A small Ludlow wall box of 1855 at St Mary's post office, Bedford. This box has no hood over the aperture and the enamelled plate is at the bottom of the door.*

LUDLOW LETTER BOXES

The pillar boxes and wall letter boxes mentioned so far were not the first letter boxes: they were preceded by ones installed at post offices. These were made at the expense of the postmaster and until the 1880s were not of any standard type, often merely taking the form of a small slot in a post office door or window.

It was not until 1895 that the Post Office undertook to pay for them and standard designs were gradually adopted. In many areas the local sub-postmaster would have got a craftsman to make a suitable letter box and many examples of these locally made boxes can still be seen.

A distinctive type of wall letter box was made particularly for sub-post offices in country areas. It is called a Ludlow, after its Birmingham manufacturer, James Ludlow. This firm supplied letter boxes from 1885 until it closed in 1965. Until the beginning of Elizabeth II's reign in 1952 the distinctive feature of these wall boxes was a large enamelled plate bearing the royal cipher and the words POST OFFICE LETTER BOX. In about 1887 similar boxes were made for sub-post offices by the Eagle Range and Foundry Company of Birmingham. They were made of wood with cast iron fronts, and in two sizes. In both versions the aperture is surrounded by the enamelled plate and

LEFT: *A large Ludlow wall box of George V. These and later Ludlows can be found with or without a collection plate set in the door, and with different styles of lettering.*

RIGHT: *The only survivor, so far as is known, of the Ludlow wall boxes made in the reign of Edward VIII. It is at Bawdsey in Suffolk.*

some boxes still have the original plate with the VR cipher, although others now have replacements with a later cipher. The apertures are either 8 inches (200 mm) or 6¼ inches (160 mm). Only some eight or nine of the larger and fifteen of the smaller boxes are still in service.

The boxes made by James Ludlow differ in two main respects: the smaller box has the enamelled plate at the bottom of the door instead of round the aperture, and neither the smaller nor the larger box has a hood over the aperture. They were also made of wood faced with sheet steel, and many have succumbed to the elements although examples of the originals can still be found. The smaller Ludlow box has the royal cipher cast above the aperture as well as on the enamelled plate, and some of the boxes with the VR cipher above the aperture now have an enamel plate with a later cipher. Both the large and small versions since the reign of George V can be found with or without a collection plate set in the door. Earlier Ludlow boxes are scarce and there is only one known survivor with the Edward VIII cipher. However, in the earlier part of 1936 some Ludlow boxes were made with the obsolete cipher of Edward VII and these are slightly larger than those made during 1901-10.

Late in 1952 the enamelled plate was abandoned and most examples with the EIIR cipher have a plain door with POST OFFICE cast on it. The type with the EIIR enamelled plate is much rarer. As with the other Post Office letter boxes, special versions with the Scottish crown have been made in Elizabeth II's reign.

LEFT: *A George VI Ludlow with collection plate and tablet at Hayfield, Derbyshire. The enamelled plate was not used after 1952 so examples with Elizabeth II's cipher are rare.*

RIGHT: *A small Ludlow wall box of Elizabeth II, after 1952, at East Chinnock, Somerset. The enamelled plate has been abandoned and the door now bears the casting POST OFFICE.*

LEFT: *The first lamp letter box of 1896 bore only the royal cipher and the word LETTERS. Only five examples survive, this one near Bethlehem, Llandeilo, Dyfed.*

RIGHT: *The second and much commoner type of Victorian lamp box has the words LETTERS ONLY above the aperture. This example is on the Fosse Way near Radford Semele, Warwickshire.*

LAMP LETTER BOXES

The type of letter box most frequently found in country areas is the lamp box, which is usually fixed to a post but sometimes set into a wall. Its great advantage is that it is cheap to produce and install, and it provides adequate posting facilities in areas where the amount of mail posted is relatively small. Lamp boxes are so called because they were originally intended to be affixed to lamp posts, which had begun to appear on the streets as public gas lighting was introduced in the nineteenth century. Local authorities were asked to approve

the proposal and in 1896 the first lamp box was made by Handyside and installed on a lamp post in Church End, Finchley, London N3. It is curious that the lamp box, which is now so widely seen in the country, had its origin in much more densely populated areas.

The earliest lamp letter boxes bore Queen Victoria's cipher and the word LETTERS, but this was soon amended to LETTERS ONLY. The first type is very rare, less than half a dozen examples being known, whilst there are over a hundred of the second type. The lamp boxes of

26

ABOVE: *Near the end of the reign of George V the lamp box was redesigned with a flatter top, larger collection plate and doorpull. These boxes are relatively uncommon.*

ABOVE RIGHT: *The 1935 design was used into the reign of George VI, the only difference being in the royal cipher. This is a type frequently seen in country areas.*

RIGHT: *A further design change was implemented in 1949 and carried on into Elizabeth II's reign. This design with the Scottish crown was erected by mistake in England — at Northford, Swindon.*

27

Edward VII can be found with the same 'open' or 'curled' royal ciphers as on pillar boxes of the same reign, the 'open' type being very much rarer. The same design of lamp box with small changes of detail was used throughout the reign of George V. Just before the end of the reign the box was completely redesigned. The top became flatter, the collection plate on the door larger; the royal cipher, displaced from the door, now appeared above the posting aperture, with LETTERS ONLY below it. There is a doorpull and the aperture is wider.

The new design was carried over into the next reign but there were persistent complaints that the aperture was still only 5½ inches (140 mm), so the lamp box was again redesigned in 1940 but because of the Second World War the new one did not appear until 1949. The box has a steel body with a separate cast iron front. The aperture, now of standard size, extends the full width of the body. The LETTERS ONLY inscription has been replaced by POST OFFICE. The curved top has gone and this design, with the Queen's cipher, is the one still used today. Changes have produced several different manufacturers' names, and, as with other types of letter box, a Scottish version was made, one or two of which have been mistakenly sited in England.

A wooden bracket box of 1883 at Pulborough station, West Sussex. The brass plate round the aperture with its inscription LONDON DISTRICT AND GENERAL POST LETTERS is missing.

The earliest mobile letter boxes were hung outside travelling post office carriages at railway stations. This example is attached to a Victorian travelling post office at the National Railway Museum in York.

MISCELLANEOUS LETTER BOXES

By 1883 a special box called a bracket box was available for use at railway stations and on board packet boats. Later they were also installed for the convenience of the staff at government offices. The boxes were made of wood and had a semicircular brass plate surrounding the aperture and bearing the words LONDON DISTRICT AND GENERAL POST LETTERS. There are examples at the stations at Machynlleth, Powys, and Pulborough, West Sussex, and at the National Postal Museum in London. What may well be a locally made version stands on Rhyl station.

The next step from the installation of letter boxes at stations was to provide them on trains. This was first done in 1882, and on payment of an extra fee letters could be posted direct into the sorting carriage of a mail train, thereby enabling letters to be posted after the last collection from the post office. At first a small wooden box was suspended from the side of the carriage, but nowadays the posting box on a travelling post office consists of a hinged flap in the side of the coach. There used to be letter boxes on some buses and trams, but none of these services seems to have survived the Second World War, although some of the mobile letter boxes can still be seen in museums.

There are many other sorts of letter boxes: main post offices have special posting boxes for first-day covers, and these are usually made of glass-reinforced plastic. Rectangular plastic boxes are also to be found in several locations, including Heathrow Airport. There are also private

LEFT: *An attractive wall letter box specially made in the reign of George V to harmonise with the frontage of Bentall's department store in Kingston-upon-Thames.*

BELOW: *This mysterious wall box with no aperture is a private one which allows letters to be posted inside the building whilst the postman can still clear the box from the street.*

ABOVE: *Pillar boxes are sometimes installed in pairs to cope with very heavy postings. In this case a specially made large concrete box has been erected at Highcliffe, Dorset.*

RIGHT: *The Type K box of 1980 is becoming more numerous. The first casting bore a commemorative plaque on the rear. This one is in Victoria Road, Swindon.*

letter boxes, which are defined as letter boxes on private premises but designed and located to the satisfaction of the Post Office. Such a box remains the property of the person owning it but the Post Office clears it subject to the payment of a fee. Many of these can be seen at hotels, large offices, factories, nursing homes and other private premises.

Letter boxes also appear in unusual colours for various reasons or with non-standard features, in picturesque locations or withdrawn from service because of damage, industrial action or redundancy. It is sometimes possible to purchase obsolete letter boxes and anyone interested should contact the local head post office.

FURTHER INFORMATION

There is little literature about letter boxes. The standard work is *The Letter Box* by Jean Farrugia, published by Centaur Press in 1969. The present author published a short *Guide to Rare British Letter Boxes* in 1985. Much more information is available by contacting the Letter Box Study Group via Mr I. G. Wilkinson, 17 Germains Close, Chesham, Buckinghamshire HP5 1JJ.